HARM POTENTIAL PROFILE

IDENTIFYING PATIENTS AT RISK FOR HARMING THEMSELVES OR OTHERS

LEWIS DONALD KITE, Ph.D.

Published by

GRAPH Publishing, L.L.C.

www.graphpublishing.com

Printed in the U.S.A.

TABLE OF CONTENTS

ABOUT THE AUTHOR
1

INTRODUCTION
3

HOW TO IDENTIFY SUICIDAL PATIENTS
5-7

THE RUTH FRY SYMBOLIC PROFILE
8-18

SUICIDAL IDEATION INDICATIONS SCALE AND INTERPRETATIONS
19-20

DRAW A PERSON AND DRAW A TREE
21-24

POTENTIAL OF HARMING OR KILLING OTHERS CHECKLIST
25-29

Psychotic Indicators in the Person Drawing 25
Hostility and Aggression in Person Drawing 26-27
Psychotic Indicators in Tree Drawing 28
Hostility and Aggression in Tree Drawing 29

DANGER TO OTHERS SCALE
30

BIBLIOGRAPHY OF REFERENCES
31-32

ABOUT THE AUTHOR

LEWIS DONALD KITE, Ph.D.

Lewis Donald Kite is the President of Kite Laboratories, Inc. in Houston, Texas. He has formally served as professor of Psychology, NASA subcontractor, and medical laboratory director. At present, he also provides consulting services to medical professionals in the field of psychiatry.

Dr. Kite received international recognition when he published a paper showing that aspirin is effective in the prevention and treatment of strokes and other vascular disorders. He is a biochemist, mental health professional, medical researcher, and inventor.

Dr. Kite has earned a doctorate in psychology as well as certificates in Art Therapy, Addictionology, Crisis Intervention Stress Management, Hypnotherapy, Neuro-Linguistic Programming, and faith-based counseling. In addition, he has completed six years of postgraduate study in analytical psychology.

Dr. Kite's inventions and tests in medicine and psychology include prescription and non-prescription medications, the Nine Item Symbolic Profile, The Harm Potential Profile, the Sexual Problems Identification Profile, and the Marriage and Family Problems Identification Profile.

Dr. Kite is available for Test Interpretations, Patient Evaluations and Counseling Assistance in regards to Test Results. He may be contacted for hire at the following:

KITE LABORATORIES, Inc.

Dr. Lewis Donald Kite, Ph.D.

Email: ldkite@aol.com

INTRODUCTION

This profile is an adjunct to the therapeutic process and is designed to help psychiatrists, other physicians and licensed mental health professionals to identify persons who are thinking of killing themselves, persons who are thinking of killing family members or others along with themselves, and potential terrorists who are thinking of killing others.

The *Harm Potential Profile* provides an insight into the patient's subconscious mind and uncovers problem areas beyond the patient's awareness. The **profile** consists of the *Ruth Fry Symbolic Profile* and the "**Draw a Person**" and "**Draw a Tree**" pages.

Our *Harm Potential Profile* was developed after years of study of art therapy, analytical psychology, and psychoanalysis. It is our sincere hope that this profile will be helpful in identifying and treating suicidal patients.

HOW TO IDENTIFY SUICIDAL PATIENTS

By Lewis D. Kite, Ph.D.

SUICIDE— A grave and non-reversible action that ends a life that might have been salvaged. It devastates family members and can have a permanently damaging effect on the therapist who has been working with the person who takes his or her own life. In her book, *Art Psychotherapy*, Harriet Wadeson states that "The feelings of therapeutic failure are seldom more acute than those of a therapist after the suicide of a client unsuspected of suicide attempt."

Even the best therapist cannot tell if a person is contemplating or intending to commit suicide by just talking to the person, unless the person or someone else tells the therapist that the person is suicidal. Most suicides catch families, friends and therapists unaware because the person intent on suicide fails to communicate his or her thoughts to anyone else.

I have talked with therapists who have suffered the trauma of a suicide of a client. They were desolated by the senseless loss of life. Typically, the therapist thinks such thoughts as, "If I had been a better therapist, I would have been able to detect suicidal tendencies." The therapist may then begin to question his or her abilities as a therapist.

I deeply sympathize with those therapists who have had to deal with a client's suicide. In all likelihood, they are highly-trained and dedicated professionals, and the tendency to blame themselves is not grounded in fact and is counterproductive. Just as a carpenter must have the right blueprints and tools to build a house, and a mechanic has to have the right equipment to repair a car, so mental health professionals must have the proper tools necessary to be able to detect and treat their patients' suicidal tendencies.

Of the patients who seek counseling, those suffering from depression are the most at risk for self-destruction. The people may be thinking about suicide but seldom voice their thoughts to their counselors. Ironically, the most dangerous time during the therapeutic process is when they seem to be doing better in therapy and are again able to make their own decisions. Unfortunately, the decisions they are making may include suicide, when all the while, the therapist may be groundlessly encouraged by the seeming success of their treatments.

In her book, *Art Psychotherapy*, Harriet Wadeson relates a story about a time when she was working in a hospital as a novice art therapist. One of the patients she was helping was a man being treated for depression who was seemingly improving, and was soon to be released to go home on weekends. Evidences of suicidal ideation appeared in his art, but the doctors and other therapists thought he was improving to the extent that it would be safe to allow him to go home for short periods of time. They believed that medications and psychotherapies were effectively treating the man's depression and disregarded Ms. Wadeson's warning about the suggestion of suicidal ideation in his drawings and her belief that, given the freedom and environmental ability, he might act on his ideas.

During the first week he was allowed to go home, he purchased a rope and some nails. The second weekend at home, he hammered the nails to a beam, fashioned a noose, and hanged himself.

We are all familiar with medical diagnostic tests that test for a variety of ailments. Physicians utilize these tools to help treat their patients. The proper tests are vital to help determine suicidal ideation if the patient does not vocalize his or her thoughts.

Traditional psychological tests cannot identify suicidal intentions if the answers to the questions asked are not meant to diagnose suicidal intentions. The only reliable way I have found to identify people who are thinking about committing suicide is to give them the Ruth Fry Symbolic Profile in conjunction with the "Draw a Person" and "Draw a Tree" parts of the H-T-P Profile by J. N. Buck in *The H-T-P Technique, Qualitative and Quantitative Scoring Manual.*

The profiles help to identify unconscious and hidden causes and contributors to a person's behavior, as well as detecting problems and problem areas that need treatment in therapy. Using the profiles decreases evaluation time and increases the success rate of treatment because they make it easier to pinpoint the causes of the person's psychological issues.

The Ruth Fry Symbolic Profile was developed by my former teacher and mentor, the late Dr. Ruth Thacker Fry, for use in counseling and psychotherapy. It consists of six squares, each containing a different symbol. The symbols are designated to elicit responses from the subconscious mind of the person, who is asked to draw pictures in each square utilizing the symbol in his or her drawing. In addition, the person is shown forty unfinished sentences and asked to complete them. The profile is intended to identify the person's feeling about himself or herself, about fantasies, relationships, religious beliefs and about his or her future.

Dr. Fry often related incidents to me and to her other students in which her profile had detected suicidal ideation in her own patients. She always utilized the profile at the beginning of therapy to help identify the hidden causes and contributors to the person's problems.

The "House, Tree, Person" Profile has been utilized successfully by therapists since J.N. Buck developed it in 1948. The profile was perfected by my former teacher, Dr. Maurice Kouguell. In his book, *DAPTH-Accessing the Unconscious in the Practice of Hypnosis and Counseling,* he gives a case example of how to identify persons with suicidal intent based upon the "draw-a-person" part of the profile. The DAPTH Profile identifies how the person feels about himself or herself, as well as relationships to family members, and can identify sexual abuse, psychic trauma, and suicidal ideas.

Drawings of nooses, tombstones, and other symbols of death show up in the drawings of the Ruth Fry Profile if the person is thinking about or planning to commit suicide. Symbols and pictures of self-anger are also important in identifying suicidal ideation in clients. The information comes to us directly from the unconscious mind in the form of pictures drawn by the client. Persons often paint a rosy picture in responding to test questions or sentence completions, but their true intent comes out when they draw the pictures as part of the profiles.

I can vouch for the effectiveness of the Ruth Fry Profile and the DAPTH Profile in identifying persons at risk for suicide. In my work as a consultant to psychiatrists, other physicians, psychotherapists, and counselors, I have personally identified several patients at risk of suicide based upon their drawings in the profiles. This enabled the physicians and therapists to get the help the persons needed to prevent their suicides. Helping to identify patients at risk of suicide so they can be prevented from committing suicide and effectively treated for their problems helps make all those years of study, research and work worthwhile.

I strongly recommend that all therapists utilize our profile with their clients as part of their testing and evaluation for several reasons. Doing so will help to identify the real hidden reasons behind a person's behavior and problem areas and can shorten the time it takes in therapy. It can also help to identify persons who are thinking about or planning to commit suicide. This profile can help you save the lives of your clients, prevent the suffering of the person's family and friends, help you to be a better therapist, as well as helping you sleep better at night knowing that you did all you knew to do to help your patients.

REFERENCES

Wadeson, H. (1980) *Art Psychotherapy*. New York. Journal of Clinical Psychology. 4, 317-396: John Wiley & Sons Publishers, 82-87.

Fry, R. T. (1976) *The Symbolic Profile*. Houston: Gulf Publishing Company.

Kouguell, M. (1994) DAPTH—Accessing the Unconscious in the Practice of Hypnosis and Counseling. Published by Dr. Maurice Kouguell, Baldwin, New York, 81-84.

Buck, J. N. (1984) The H-T-P Technique, a Qualitative and Quantitative scoring Manual. *Journal of Clinical Psychology*. 4, 317-396.

THE RUTH FRY SYMBOLIC PROFILE

The Ruth Fry Symbolic Profile has been a valuable counseling aid for over thirty years.

The profile quickly identifies the patient's problems.

There are no right or wrong responses to the profile.

The Ruth Fry Symbolic Profile—Instructions for administration to patients:

1. First, give the patient a copy of page 9 of the profile. Instruct the patient to draw a picture in each of the boxes of the profile using the symbols in the boxes on pages 10 through 15. Then instruct them to label each box in the profile, naming the picture they drew using the specified symbols.

2. Second, when this exercise is completed, instruct the patient to complete each sentence on pages 17-18 with quick, first responses.

THE RUTH FRY SYMBOLIC PROFILE

Name_____   Date_____

Sex_____   Age_____

Marital status: M S D W

Directions:

1. Draw something in each square below using the symbol presented. Label each square.
2. After the pictures are completed, finish the sentences on the next pages using the key words with a quick, first response.

EGO SQUARE

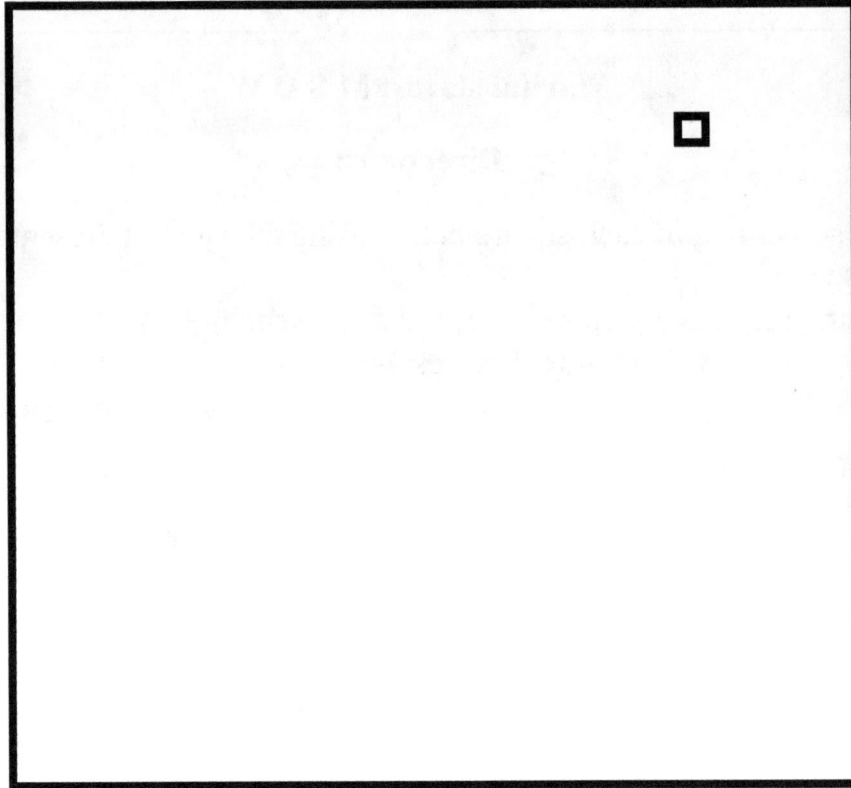

The "EGO" symbol in square #1 elicits from the unconscious of the person drawing the picture thoughts about what he or she thinks and feels about him/herself and his or her self-image. Symbols of death in this square indicate a desire to commit suicide.

"The symbol in the Ego Square (#1) is the quaternary, a small square, an earth form, having to do with the maternal and passive. The ego forms the center of the field of consciousness, and in so far as this comprises the empirical personality, the ego is the subject of all personal acts of consciousness. The Ego is the means by which adaptation to outward reality is experienced." (Fry, 1976)

FANTASY SQUARE

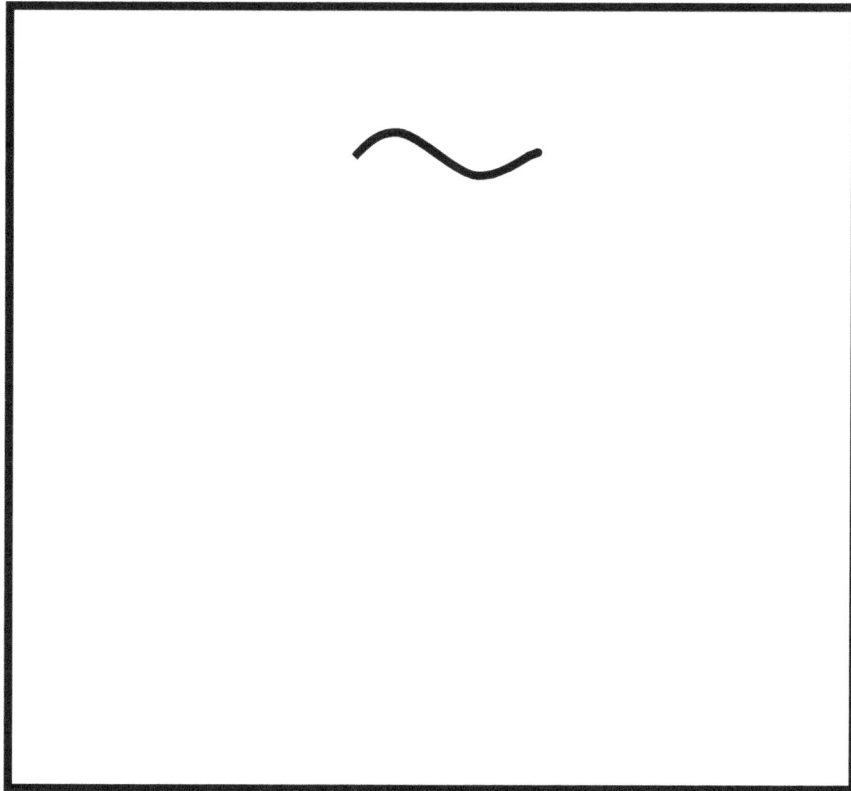

The "FANTASY" symbol in square #2 elicits fantasies from the unconscious mind of the person. The drawing represents the fantasy life of the individual and what he/she would like to do or be. Symbols of death in this picture indicate a fantasy to commit suicide.

"The wavy line in the Fantasy Square (#2) is a symbol of air and could represent imaginative thoughts or ideas floating around, or the possibilities of solutions which are still up in the air. These would be elusive, indefinite contents of the unconscious." (Fry, 1976)

FAMILY SQUARE

The "FAMILY" symbol, #3, elicits from the unconscious mind of the person drawing the picture thoughts about his or her family and about the relationship to his/her family. The patient expresses his/her place in the family and the relationship to his/her family. Symbols of death in the picture are an indication of the person harming members of his/her family.

"The 'unity of origin' symbol, a small dot, is in the Family Square (#3). The family is the most instinctive, fundamental social, or mating, group—the seed of individual origin. This social unit is the first place in which we begin to experience ourselves in relationship to others." (Fry, 1976)

SELF-DETERMINATION SQUARE

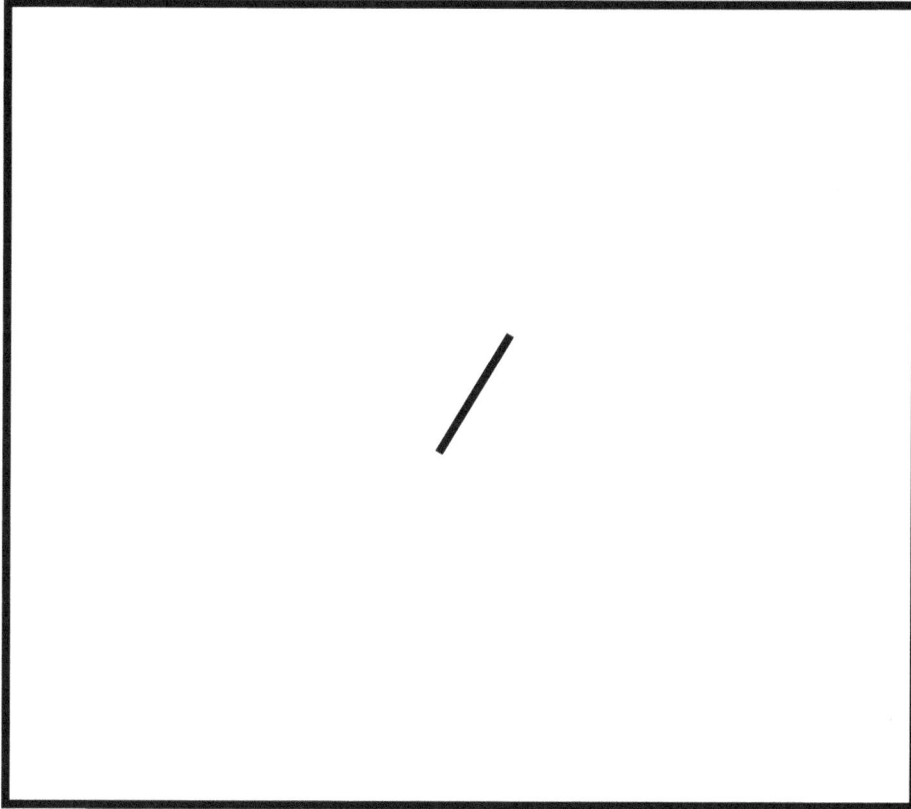

The "SELF-DETERMINATION" symbol in square #4 elicits from the unconscious the patient's aspirations and how he/she wants to change him/herself. Symbols of death in this picture indicate a determination to commit suicide.

"The Self-Determination Square (#4) with the diagonal line contains the symbol for the 'active dynamic principle.' The development of the diagonal line would be an indication of the person's search for direction in life." (Fry,1976)

RELIGION SQUARE

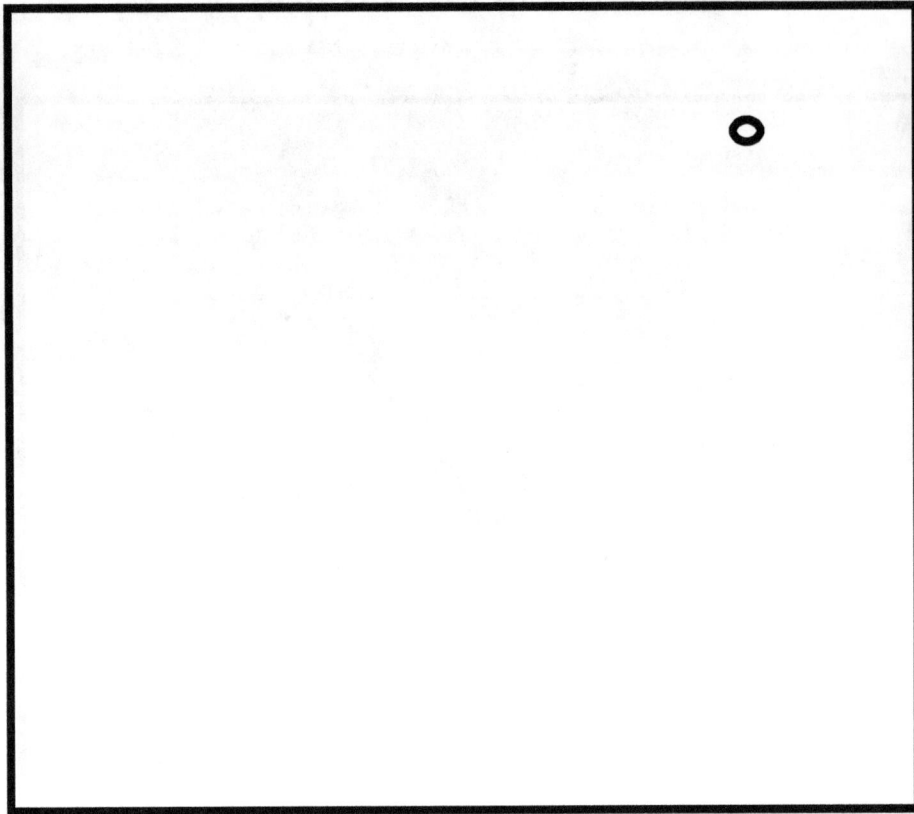

The "RELIGION" symbol in square #5 elicits from the unconscious what the person thinks about religion and God.

"The symbol in the Religion Square (#5) represents infinity, the universe, the Almighty. The symbol would help to express the universal, instinctive need to be in touch with that which is more than we. The relationship, or lack of relationship, to a god-image, either personal or impersonal, is where we seek the ultimate meaning of life. From our perception of this image, reflecting life's meaning, we derive our ethical behavior and/or moral attitudes." (Fry, 1976)

POTENTIAL SQUARE

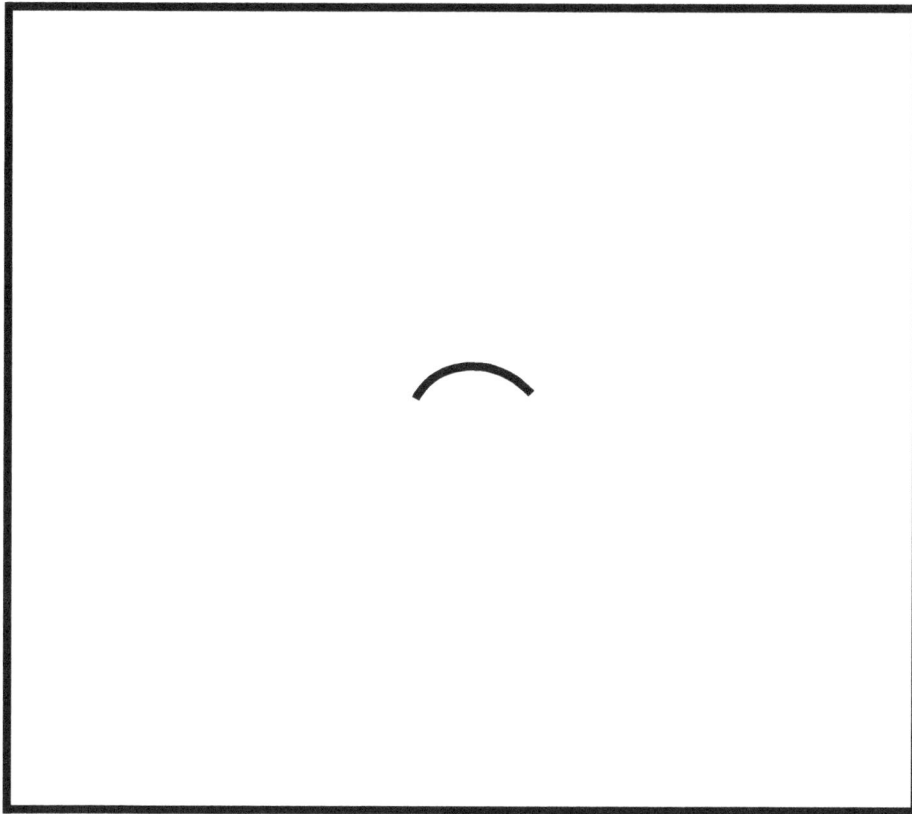

The "POTENTIAL" symbol, #6, elicits from the unconscious what the patient thinks will become of him/her in the future. Symbols of death in the picture indicate future plans for violence.

"The arc in the Potential Square (#6) is part of a circle. The circle symbolizes wholeness, denotes the totality of the personality. The symbol is left open on the profile for the purpose of stimulating the person to find his/her own potential." (Fry, 1976)

THE VALUE OF SENTENCE COMPLETIONS

The sentence completions can be utilized by the therapist to identify the problems, desires, feeling, and relationships of the patient. They are also useful in identifying persons who may be a danger to themselves or to others. Sentence completions containing threats toward the self, the person's family, or other people should be noted and addressed in therapy.

Do not overlook the good things in the person's life that the person notes in the sentence completions. One technique that works wonders is to discuss at the end of each session one of the good things that the person likes that they have disclosed in the sentence completions. This helps keep the emphasis on positive, rather than negative, comments and promotes feelings of hope and well-being.

Discussing something good in the person's life will also make him or her want to return for further therapy since the patient feels good talking about pleasant ideas, experiences, people, or things with the therapist. It only takes a few minutes at the end of each session to discuss with the patient what he or she likes or loves with the therapist. The therapist may be pleasantly surprised at the results.

SYMBOLIC PROFILE SENTENCE COMPLETIONS

1. I like _____

2. I want _____

3. My family _____

4. I must _____

5. Church is _____

6. I hope _____

7. I love _____

8. I feel _____

9. Children are _____

10. People think of me _____

11. God _____

12. I often _____

13. I hate _____

14. Someday I _____

15. My father _____

16. I cannot _____

17. I fear _____

18. I wish _____

19. I failed _____

20. My greatest success _____

21. My mother _____

22. I need _____

23. I believe _____

24. My worst fault _____

25. Women _____

26. Love _____

27. Sisters are _____

28. I regret _____

29. I was happiest when _____

30. People _____

31. Men _____

32. Sex _____

33. At home _____

34. I miss _____

35. I think _____

36. Marriage _____

37. Brothers _____

38. A spouse _____

39. I think of myself as _____

40. My dreams _____

SUICIDAL IDEATION INDICATIONS SCALE AND INTERPRETATIONS

Check those indicators that appear in the drawings.

SYMBOLS OF DEATH OR WEAPONS IN THE RUTH FRY PROFILE:

1. _____**Ego Square (#1) with symbols of <u>death</u>**
   Interpretation: Symbols of death in this square indicate suicidal thinking.

2. _____**Ego Square (#1) with picture of a <u>weapon or weapons</u>**
   Interpretation: These may indicate either a desire to harm themselves or others, and/or a desire to commit suicide.

3. _____**Fantasy Square (#2) with symbol of <u>death</u>**
   Interpretation: The presence of a symbol of death indicates a fantasy to commit suicide.

4. _____**Fantasy Square (#2) with a picture of <u>weapon or weapons</u> Interpretation:** The presence of a weapon or weapons may indicate a fantasy about harming themselves and/or others.

5. _____**Family Square (#3) with <u>weapons or weapons</u>**
   Interpretation: The presence of these symbols indicates a desire to harm or kill one or more family members.

6. _____**Family Square (#3) with <u>weapon or weapons</u>**
   Interpretation: The presence of a weapon or weapons indicates a desire to harm or kill one or more family members.

7. _____**Self-Determination Square (#4) with symbol of <u>death</u>**
   Interpretation: The presence of symbols of death here indicates that the person is planning to commit suicide.

8. _____**Self-Determination Square (#4) with a picture of a <u>weapon or weapons</u> Interpretation:** The presence of weapons may indicate thinking about harming oneself or others.

9. _____**Religion Square (#5) with the symbol of death or <u>weapons</u> Interpretation:** The presence of these symbols may indicate a connection between violence and death and the patient's religion. The presence of weapons and/or symbols of death in this square can indicate that the person may be a potential terrorist and may be planning to kill others.
(A profile of a potential terrorist would show weapons and/or symbols of death in the Religion Square, as well as showing similar indications in our section on <u>Identifying persons who are a danger to others</u>.)

10. _____**Potential Square (#6) with symbol of <u>death</u> Interpretation:** The presence of these symbols in this square indicates that the person is planning on committing suicide in the future.

"DRAW A PERSON" AND "DRAW A TREE"

"The 'Draw-a-Person' page reflects what the subject would like to be, his attitude toward interpersonal relationships, special fears, and beliefs, and how he sees himself in the environment. It offers a psychological and physiological overall impression of the subject." (Kouguell, 1994)

"The drawing that a patient makes of a human figure represents the self in the environment. The actual presentation of the self may reflect the patient's deepest wishes; it may reflect and expose a painful psychical or emotional deficit; it may be a vigorous compensation for this defect or a combination of all the factors." (Handler, 1985)

"The tree arouses more subconscious and unconscious associations. It frequently is a projection of the individual's experience and resources. The tree also represents the growth, energy level and feeling of interpersonal balance. It is a reflection of a self-portrait." (Buck, 1948)

ADMINISTRATION OF THE "DRAW A PERSON" AND "DRAW A TREE" TO PATIENTS

1. First, give the patient a copy of the "Draw a Person" page and instruct him or her to draw a person on the page.
2. When that activity has been completed, give the patient a copy of the "Draw a Tree" page and instruct him or her to draw a tree on that page.

Name_____Age_____Sex_____

DRAW A PERSON IN THE SPACE BELOW

Name_____Age_____Sex_____

DRAW A TREE IN THE SPACE BELOW

POTENTIAL OF HARMING OR KILLING OTHERS CHECKLIST

PSYCHOTIC & AGGRESSIVE/HOSTILE INDICATIONS:

<u>PSYCHOTIC INDICATIONS: PERSON DRAWING</u>

Check those indicators present in the drawing:

1. _____ Peripheral lines treated with heavy pressure in the drawing or drawings indicate psychotic features (Kouguell, 1994).

2. _____ A person seemingly on tip toe in the drawing indicates psychotic features (Kouguell, 1994).

3. _____ Drawing the person off-balance and falling over indicates loss of contact with reality (Kouguell, 1994).

4. _____ Transparency in a drawing indicates psychotic features (Kouguell, 1994).

5. _____ Figure pictured at 15% or more off balance indicates possible instability, mental imbalance (Kouguell, 1994).

6. _____ Neck omitted indicates inadequate impulse control (Kougell, 1994).

7. _____ Shoulders unequal indicates emotional instability (Kougell, 1994).

AGGRESSIVE & HOSTILE INDICATIONS: <u>PERSON DRAWING</u>

Check those indicators present in the drawing:

8. _____ Head too big in relation to size of body indicates aggression (Kougell, 1994).

9. _____ Paper turning by person indicates aggression and hostility (Jolee, 1964).

10. _____ Pronounced shading in drawing indicates aggression and hostility (Buck, 1969; Wolk, 1969).

11. _____ Violent movements in pictures indicate possible aggression (Allen, 1959).

12. _____ Drawing conspicuously too large for paper indicates aggression and hostility (Kouguell, 1994).

13. _____ Hair well outlined, but shaded indicates aggression and hostility (Kouguell, 1994).

14. _____ Mouth with sneer indicates hostility (McElhaney, 1969).

15. _____ Eyes closed indicates repressed hostility (Schldprout Etal, 1972).

16. _____ Eyebrows frowning indicates possibility hostility (McElhaney, 1969).

17. _____ Nostrils showing indicates aggressive tendencies (Kouguell, 1994).

18. _____ Chin enlarged indicates aggressive tendencies and indicates compensation for feelings of weakness (Kouguell, 1994).

19. _____ Arms folded indicates possible hostility (Buck, 1950).

20. _____ Person represented in a threatening attitude indicates aggression and hostility (Kouguell, 1994).

21. _____ Shading on arms indicates aggressive impulses (Kouguell, 1994).

22. _____ Closed fists indicates repressed aggression (Kouguell, 1994).

23. _____ Gloves indicate possible difficulty in controlling emotions (Machover, 1949).

24. _____ Feet sharply pointed indicates possible hostility (Jacks, 1969).

25. _____ Sharply pointed toes indicates aggression and hostility (Kouguell, 1994).

26. _____ Fingers long and spike-like indicates aggressive and hostile (Kouguell, 1994).

27. _____ Large fingers indicate tendency to be assaultive (Kouguell, 1994).

28. _____ Fingers to the left in adults indicates the tendency to be aggressive in an infantile manner (Machover, 1949).

29. _____ Shoulders sharply squared indicates overly defensive and hostile to others (Kouguell, 1994).

30. _____ Shoulders very broad indicates possible aggression (Levy, 1950).

PSYCHOTIC INDICATIONS: <u>TREE DRAWING</u>

Check those indicators present in the drawing:

31. _____ Grotesque picture indicates serious psychological instability (Allen, 1958).

32. _____ A mutilated tree and the use of degrading details underscores the patient's hostility (Kouguell, 1994).

33. _____ Drawing the tree as if off-balance and falling often means psychotic loss of contact with reality (Kouguell, 1994).

34. _____ Tree with open base suggests inadequate reality contact on the part of the subject to a smaller extent (Kouguell, 1994).

35. _____ Overemphasis upon roots which enter the ground - implies a great need to maintain a grasp on reality (Kouguell, 1994).

36. _____ Peripheral lines on the tree treated with heavy pressure in the drawing indicates a psychotic condition (Kouguell, 1994).

HOSTILITY & AGGRESSION INDICATIONS: <u>TREE DRAWING</u>

Check those indicators present in the drawing:

37. _____ Tree extremely large indicates aggressive tendencies (Kouguell, 1994).

38. _____ Two-dimensional branches drawn resembling clubs or sharply pointed branches indicates hostility and aggression (Kouguell, 1994).

39. _____ A mutilated tree underscores patient hostility (Kouguell, 1994).

40. _____ Drawing conspicuously too large for the page indicates aggression (Kouguell, 1994).

41. _____ Tree which consists of a looping line representing the tree's branch structure, and two vertical lines closed or unclosed at the trunk's base indicates strong hostile impulses (Kouguell, 1994).

42. _____ Tree shading excessively dark indicates aggression and hostility behavior (Kouguell, 1994).

43. _____ Growth at bottom of tree indicates aggression with nothing to look forward to (Kouguell, 1994).

44. _____ Tree extremely large indicates aggressive tendencies (Kouguell, 1994).

45. _____ Branches drawn looking like spikes indicates hostile and aggressive tendencies (Mussell, 1969).

46. _____ Bark heavily drawn indicates hostility and anxiety (Buck, 1966).

DANGER TO OTHERS SCALE

Check these indicators that appear in the drawings:

_____1		_____24	
_____2		_____25	
_____3		_____26	
_____4		_____27	
_____5		_____28	
_____6		_____29	
_____7		_____30	
_____8		_____31	
_____9		_____32	
_____10		_____33	
_____11		_____34	
_____12		_____35	
_____13		_____36	
_____14		_____37	
_____15		_____38	
_____16		_____39	
_____17		_____40	
_____18		_____41	
_____19		_____42	
_____20		_____43	
_____21		_____44	
_____22		_____45	
_____23		_____46	

TOTAL HOSTILITY/AGGRESSION INDICATORS   **OUT OF 46**

 # OF THREATS TO OTHERS IN THE SENTENCE COMPLETIONS = _____
INTERPRETATION: The greater the number of psychotic indicators, hostility/aggression indicators, and threats to others in the sentence completions, the greater the chance of the patient harming others.

BIBLIOGRAPHY OF REFERENCES

Allen, R.M. (1958) *Personal Assessment Procedures.* New York: Harper.

Buck, J.N. (1948). The H-T-P technique; a qualitative and quantitative scoring manual. *Journal of Clinical Psychology, 4,* 317-396.

Buck, J.N. (1950) *Administration & Interpretation of the H-T-P Test: Proceedings of the H-T-P workshop held at Veterans Administration Hospital.* Richmond, Virginia: Psychological Services.

Buck, J.M. (1966) *The House-Tree-Person Technique: Revised Manual,* Los Angeles: Western Psychological Services.

Buck, J.M. (1969) The use of the H-T-P in the investigation of intrafamilial conflict. In J.N. Buck & E.F. Hammer, *Advances and applications,* Los Angeles: Western Psychological Services.

Fry, Ruth Thacker. (1976) *The Symbolic Profile.* Houston, Texas: Gulf Publishing Company.

Handler, L & Reyher, J. (1965) Figure drawing anxiety indices: A review of the literature. *Journal of Projective Techniques.* 29, 305-313.

Jacks, I. (1969) The Clinical Application of the H-T-P in Criminological Settings. In J. N. Buck and E. F. Hammer (Eds) in *Advances in the House - tree - person technique: Variations and Applications.* Los Angeles: Western Psychological Services, 1969.

Jolles, I. (1964) *A Catalogue for the Quantitative Interpretation of H-T-P (Revised).* Los Angeles: Western Psychological Services.

Kouguell, M. (1994) *Dapth: Assessing the Unconscious in the Practice of Hypnosis and Counseling.*

Levy, S. (1950) Figure Drawing as a Projective Test. In L'Abat. & LL Bellak (Eds.) *Projective Psychology.* New York: Knopf. 257-297.

Machover, K. (1949) *Personality Projection in the Drawings of the Human Figure Drawings.* Springfield, Illinois: Charles C. Thomas Press.

McElhaney, M. (1969) *Clinical Psychological Assessment of the Human Figure Drawing.* Springfield, Illinois: Charles C. Thomas Press.

Mersell, G. R. (1969) The use of the H-T-P with the Mentally Deficient. In J. N. Buck & E. F. Hammer (Eds.) *Advances in the House - Tree- Person- Technique: Variations and Applications.* Los Angeles: Western Psychological Services.

Schildkrout, M.S., Shemper, I. R. & Sonnenblick, M. (1972) *Human Figure Drawings in Adolescents.* New York: Brunner/Mazel Publishers.

Wolk, R.L. (1969) Projective Drawings (H-T-P) of Aged People. In J. N. Buck & E. F. Hammer, (Eds.) *Advances in the House - Tree- Person Technique: Variations and Applications.* Los Angeles: Western Psychological Services.

www.ingramcontent.com/pod-product-compliance
Lightning Source LLC
Chambersburg PA
CBHW080632030426
42336CB00018B/3170